The Wisdom of Donald Trump: A Book of Quotations

W. E. Smith

ISBN: 9798673602683

CONTENTS

ABOUT THIS BOOK

This book is a collection of excerpts from transcriptions of various speeches, addresses, and interviews given by Donald J. Trump.

ON SPACE

Moments ago, as we witnessed the launch of two great American astronauts into space, we were filled with the sense of pride and unity that brings us together as Americans. That same spirit which powered our astronauts to the Moon has also helped lift our country to ever greater heights of justice and opportunity throughout our history. So today, as we mark a renewed commitment to America's future in space, a tremendous commitment it is. Let us also commit to a brighter future for all of our citizens right here on Earth. When Americans are united, there is nothing we cannot do.

Speech at the Kennedy Space Center, May 30, 2020

ON OPTIMISM

Fear and doubt is not a good thought process because this is a time for tremendous hope and joy and optimism and action. But to embrace the possibilities of tomorrow, we must reject the perennial prophets of doom and their predictions of the apocalypse. They are the heirs of yesterday's foolish fortune-tellers -- and I have them and you have them, and we all have them, and they want to see us do badly, but we don't let that happen. They predicted an overpopulation crisis in the 1960s, mass starvation in the '70s, and an end of oil in the 1990s. These alarmists always demand the same thing: absolute power to dominate, transform, and control every aspect of our lives. We will never let radical socialists destroy our economy, wreck our country, or eradicate our liberty. America will always be the proud, strong, and unyielding bastion of freedom. In America, we understand what the pessimists refuse to see: that a growing and vibrant market economy focused on the future lifts the human spirit and excites creativity strong enough to overcome any challenge -- any challenge by far.

Speech at the World Economic Forum, January 21, 2020

ON FEDERAL JUDGES

Republicans are the party of liberty, equality, and justice for all. We are the party of Abraham Lincoln and we are the party of law and order. Think of what we've done. We will have close to 300 federal judges appointed and approved by the end of my first time. That's an all-time record. That's an all-time record. I've always heard how important judges are. Now we know how important they are. Think of that, over 300, around 300 by the end of the term. And when we have another four years, we're going to have a big, big percentage of the total number. Very important, November 3rd and two great Supreme Court judges. So, we have two justices of the Supreme Court. Justice Gorsuch, Justice Kavanaugh, they're great. They are -- they're great. We have two and we could get a few more. Yeah. We could get a few. We've spent over $2 trillion to completely rebuild the unmatched strength and power of the United States military and all of that incredible equipment, whether it's submarines or missiles or rockets or jet fighters, bombers, it's all built in the USA.

Speech at political rally in Tulsa, Oklahoma, June 20, 2020

ON CLIMATE CHANGE

You can't use hairspray because hairspray is going to affect the ozone. I'm trying to figure out. Let's see, I'm in my room in New York City and I want to put a little spray so that I can, right? But I hear, well, they don't want me to use hairspray. They want me to use the pump because the other one, which I really like better than going bing, bing, bing. And then it comes out in big globs, right? And it's stuck in your hair and you say, Oh my God, I gotta take a shower again. My hair is all screwed up, right? I want to use hairspray. They say don't use hairspray. It's bad for the ozone. So I'm sitting at this concealed apartment. This concealed -- you know, I really do live in a very nice apartment, right? But it's sealed. It's beautiful. I don't think anything gets out. And I'm not supposed to be using hairspray. But think of it, so Obama's always talking about the global warming, that global warming is our biggest and most dangerous problem, OK? No, no, think of it. I mean even if you're a believer in global warming, ISIS is a big problem. Russia is a problem. China is a problem. We get a lot of problems. By the way, the maniac in North Korea is a problem. He actually has nuclear weapons, right? That's a problem. We get a lot of problems. We got a lot of problems. That's right. We don't win anymore. He said, we want to win. We don't win anymore. We're gonna win a lot. If I get elected, we're gonna win a lot. We're gonna win so much. We're going to win a lot. We're going to win so much you're all going to get sick and tired of winning years. You'll say, oh no, not again. I'm only kidding. You never get tired of winning, right? Never. But think of it. So Obama is talking about all of this with the global warming and that and a lot of it's a hoax. It's a hoax. I mean it's a moneymaking industry. OK? It's a hoax. A lot of it. Look, I want clean air and want clean water. That's my global -- I want clean clean crystal water and I want clean air and we can do that, but we

don't have to destroy our businesses. We don't have to

destroy it, OK? And by the way, China isn't abiding by anything. They're buying all of our coal. We can't use coal anymore, essentially. They're buying our coal and they're using it. Now when you talk about the planet, it's so big out there. We're here, they're there. It's like they're our next door neighbor, right, in terms of the universe. Miss Universe, by the way, made a great deal when I sold. Oh did I get rich. That was a great deal huh. You know they broke my choppers on that. They said, he talks about illegal immigration. We're not going to put him on television. First of all, that Univision is being sued like crazy. You wouldn't believe it. And NBC made a great deal with them, just like an amazing deal. Far more than I would have ever gotten. I mean, I made an unbelievable deal far more than I ever would have gotten if I said, I think I'm going to sell it if times were normal, right? Isn't it amazing the way this is gonna work out. But I love Miss Universe and I love the universe.

Speech at political rally in Hilton Head, SC, December 30, 2015

ON WINDMILLS

I never understood wind. You know, I know windmills very much. I've studied it better than anybody I know. It's very expensive. They're made in China and Germany mostly — very few made here, almost none. But they're manufactured - tremendous, if you're into this — tremendous fumes. Gases are spewing into the atmosphere. You know we have a world, right? So the world is tiny compared to the universe. So tremendous, tremendous amount of fumes and everything. You talk about the carbon footprint — fumes are spewing into the air. Right? Spewing. Whether it's in China, Germany, it's going into the air. It's our air, their air, everything — right?

Speech at Turning Point USA Student Action Summit,
December 21, 2019

ON COVID-19 TESTING

To be specific, COVID-19, that name gets further and further away from China as opposed to calling it the Chinese virus. And despite the fact that we -- I have done a phenomenal job with it. I shut down the United States to a very heavily infected, but all people from China in late January, which is months earlier than other people would have done it, if they would have done it at all. I saved hundreds of thousands of lives. We don't ever get even a mention. Then, I closed it down to Europe early, closed it down because I saw what was happening. And by the way, most people said, don't do it, don't do it. We saved hundreds of thousands of lives and all we do is get hit on like we're terrible. And what we've done with the ventilators and with the medical equipment and with testing -- you know, testing is a double edged sword. We've tested now 25 million people. It's probably 20 million people more than anybody else. Germany's done a lot, South Korea's done a lot. They call me, they say the job you're doing -- here's the bad part, when you test of -- when you do testing to that extent, you're going to find more people, you're going to find more cases. So, I said to my people slow the testing down, please. They test and they test. We had tests that people don't know what's going on. We got tests. We got another one over here, the young man's 10 years old. He's got the sniffles. He's recover in about 15 minutes. That's the case. That's the case.

Speech at political rally in Tulsa, Oklahoma, June 20, 2020

ON VENTILATORS

The company founded by a man named Henry Ford -- good bloodlines, good bloodlines, if you believe in that stuff. You got good blood. They teamed up with the company founded by Thomas Edison -- that's General Electric. It's good stuff. That's good stuff. And you put it all together. They're all looking down right now and they'd be very proud of what they see. You began the production of 50,000 lifesaving ventilators, a number that, if you go back just two months, I would say -- most people would say it would be impossible to believe. The media is back there and they would have said, a couple of months ago, the creation of that many ventilators would have been not a possible thing. Every single one of these ventilators is made in the USA, with American heart, American hands, and American pride. Just as your great grandparents produced more than one Model T every minute, just as your grandmothers and grandfathers produced a B-24. You did the B-24 bombers. I saw pictures in the back. That was quite a weapon. That was quite an incredible weapon -- B-24 bomber. And just as a Ford F-150 normally drives off the line every 52 seconds, you quickly mastered this complex new machine. A ventilator is a very complicated, delicate, big, expensive machine. One month ago, Ford had never built a single ventilator. And now you're a world leader. That's not bad. You adopted the designs of a company that was building just 10 a week, but a very high-quality ventilator. And very soon you'll be producing one new ventilator every single minute. It's an absolute amazing achievement and you're really helping now, beyond the country; you're helping other countries throughout the world. We have 188 countries that are fighting this terrible enemy. And ventilators are something they could never -- you can do cotton swabs, you can do all of the things. You can even do testing. But ventilators are a whole different lot. It's very tough. Great job. Thanks to you, we'll stockpile over 100,000 new ventilators in the next few months. And I've offered over 14,000 to friends and allies all around the world, and they desperately need them. Just this week, I spoke to five countries. They call me -- is it possible to get ventilators to them. And I'm sending them over.

Speech at a Ford Plant in Ypsilanti, Michigan, May 21, 2020

ON MERRY CHRISTMAS

Things were looking very bleak, even a thing like Merry Christmas. Remember? I used to go around in December. I'd say, we're going to say Christmas again. We're going to say Christmas again. And now, they're all saying Merry Christmas again, right? They're all saying it. You go to these big department stores three years ago, four years ago, and they'd have the snow and they'd have the red and the white. They'd have everything, but they wouldn't say Christmas. I said, where's Merry Christmas and they said, we can't say it. They're all saying it again. They're saying it proudly. Evangelicals, Christians of every denomination and believers of every faith have never had a greater champion, not even close, in the White House than you have right now.

Address to the Evangelicals for Trump in Miami, January 3, 2020

ON RELIGION AND SOCIETY

A society without religion cannot prosper. A nation without faith cannot endure because justice, goodness, and peace cannot prevail without the glory of Almighty God. You know that very well. You know that very well. For America to thrive in the 21st century, we must renew faith and family as the center of American life. There are those who say these sacred beliefs are outdated, but we know they are just the opposite. Our traditions and our values are timeless and immortal. They don't know what they're missing, right? They don't know what they're missing. Our faith is needed now more than ever while certain fads come and go. It's an eternal truth that faith and family lead to the stability, happiness, and prosperity of nations.

Address to the Evangelicals for Trump in Miami, January 3, 2020

ON CHICAGO

It's embarrassing to us as a nation. All over the world, they're talking about Chicago. Afghanistan is a safe place by comparison. It's true. Police officers of Chicago are entitled to a police superintendent who has their backs and knows what he's doing. You're entitled to a police superintendent who sides with you, with the people of Chicago -- the people want this -- and with the families of Chicago, not the criminals and the gang members that are here illegally, and not the stupid politicians that have no idea what the hell they're doing. But I'm going to tell you a quick story because it happened right here. And I was very impressed with a certain person, whoever that person may be. I'm sure that we could find him. But about three years ago, I was leaving Chicago, and I was accompanied by a massive motorcycle brigade of policemen. And to do that, they have to volunteer, because, I guess, most places say you have to volunteer. Well, I had a lot of volunteers, I'll tell you. Hundreds and hundreds of them. Other candidates have none. It's almost like a free poll. I had hundreds of them. Chicago was in the news a lot, just like it is now, because of all of the killings going on and all of the shooting and all of the horrible things happening. When I arrived at the airplane, the police officers asked whether or not it would be possible to have some pictures. And before I won the election, I could do that. I would do that routinely. Now I think Secret Service has a little bit of a problem. If it was up to me, I'd do it. But it was just before -- might've even been President-elect. Wasn't long ago. The leader of the brigade was this really powerful, strong-looking guy. A big booming voice. And he was definitely the boss. Do we know what that means? He was the boss. "Put your cycles over here. Come on, let's go. He's going to take a picture. Come on, let's go. Hurry up. Come on." And yet, they all loved him. They love Vince Lombardi. They love Belichick. Right? They love Coach Belichick. They love certain people. It's called "respect." But he was very respectfully shouting at his men, and -- "Come on, let's go." And they were doing exactly as he said. He was the guy. Just as I'm boarding the plane, I asked this man -- I had a lot of respect for him myself because I saw the way he was -- he wasn't doing anything wrong; he was just the boss, who is a respected person. I said, "Excuse me. Come here. What the hell is happening in Chicago"? And he said, "It's very sad, sir. Very, very sad. I hate to see what's going on. I love this city so much. I hate it." I asked him, "What do you think the problem is"? And he said, "There's no leadership from the Mayor and there's none at the top of the police department. They're afraid to do anything." He said, "We have great police, sir. The best in the country." And you all feel that about your own police. But he said that. He said, "But we don't have the leadership at the top. It's so sad." I said, "You're a tough guy. How long do you think it would take you to fix this killing problem in Chicago?" He looked at me, he said, "One day, sir. These cops are great. They know all the bad guys, sir. They know exactly what to do. We could straighten it out so quickly that your head would spin." I left very impressed. Whether it was one day, one week, or one month, there was no doubt he could've done it. And I actually told the story numerous times, and I actually sent his name in to somebody involved with Chicago. And that's the last time I ever heard of that man. He's probably got a good job someplace, outside of a police force. I'm sorry to do that to you, but he's -- he's happy. He's happy. Because he doesn't have to put up with the nonsense that you have to put up with. But I thought, "There's a guy who could be your police superintendent and do a hell of a job." He'd straighten things out. So that was years ago. And I was just thinking about it. I just thought about it on the trip over. I said, "You know, I'm going to Chicago and I want to tell the story," because it was, to me, a great story. Because you could fix this up so fast. Good leadership would be pretty easy to find.

Speech at the International Association of Chiefs of Police, October 28, 2019

ON A SECOND TERM

Well, one of the things that will be really great, you know, the word experience is still good. I always say talent is more important than experience. I've always said that. But the word experience is a very important word. It's an, a very important meaning. I never did this before. I never slept over in Washington. I was in Washington, I think, 17 times. All of a sudden, I'm president of the United States. You know the story. I'm riding down Pennsylvania Avenue with our first lady and I say, 'This is great,'" But I didn't know very many people in Washington, it wasn't my thing. I was from Manhattan, from New York. Now, I know everybody, and I have great people in the administration. You make some mistakes. Like, you know, an idiot like Bolton. The only thing he wanted to do was drop bombs on everybody. You don't have to drop bombs on everybody. You don't have to kill people.

Interview with Sean Hannity, June 25, 2020

ON THE ECONOMY

You know, interestingly, we're a free trade country, but it's not really free trade. If you look at what's going on with the manipulation of other currencies, especially and in particular China. But free trade is OK if you have really smart leadership. When your leadership isn't up to par, when your leadership isn't smart, when, in some cases, your leadership is incompetent, free trade is really bad for us. Believe me. Because we're on the wrong end of the stick. So when I look at what's going on with this country, when I look at $17 trillion, a word that you didn't even hear 10 years ago, the word trillion, it didn't exist as far as we were concerned. Now, that's all you hear, $17 trillion in debt. You look at deficits that are record setting, and they're not going to get better. The market is false. You know, about two years ago, I said I'm going to invest in the stock market. I was never a stock market person. But the market had to go up based on what they're doing with the Federal Reserve. It almost had to go up. I don't even consider it a great threat. And I've made a lot of money in the stock market because I said the market has to go up. They're giving you free money. But that's a false economy. And I better not speak too much about that because otherwise I have to sell my stock very quickly. But it's sort of a false economy. It's not real.

Speech in Ames, Iowa, August 10, 2013

ON AMERICA'S FOUNDERS

There could be no better place to celebrate America's independence than beneath this magnificent, incredible, majestic mountain and monument to the greatest Americans who have ever lived. Today, we pay tribute to the exceptional lives and extraordinary legacies of George Washington, Thomas Jefferson, Abraham Lincoln, and Teddy Roosevelt. I am here as your President to proclaim before the country and before the world: This monument will never be desecrated, these heroes will never be defaced, their legacy will never, ever be destroyed, their achievements will never be forgotten, and Mount Rushmore will stand forever as an eternal tribute to our forefathers and to our freedom. We gather tonight to herald the most important day in the history of nations: July 4th, 1776.

At those words, every American heart should swell with pride. Every American family should cheer with delight. And every American patriot should be filled with joy, because each of you lives in the most magnificent country in the history of the world, and it will soon be greater than ever before. Our Founders launched not only a revolution in government, but a revolution in the pursuit of justice, equality, liberty, and prosperity. No nation has done more to advance the human condition than the United States of America. And no people have done more to promote human progress than the citizens of our great nation. It was all made possible by the courage of 56 patriots who gathered in Philadelphia 244 years ago and signed the Declaration of Independence. They enshrined a divine truth that changed the world forever when they said: "... all men are created equal." These immortal words set in motion the unstoppable march of freedom. Our Founders boldly declared that we are all endowed with the same divine rights -- given [to] us by our Creator in Heaven. And that which God has given us, we will allow no one, ever, to take away -- ever. Seventeen seventy-six represented the culmination of thousands of years of western civilization and the triumph not only of spirit, but of wisdom, philosophy, and reason.

Speech at a Fourth of July Fireworks Show at Mount Rushmore, July 3, 2020

ON IMMIGRATION

We have many problems in our country. One of them is immigration. Now I took a tremendous hit when I brought up illegal immigration when announced I was running for president. And for two weeks I said, you know, Rush Limbaugh is a great guy, he said, he has suffered more incoming, meaning the press than anybody I've seen. So what happened is you have now found out what illegal immigration is all about, and I am so happy that I'm the one that brought it to the fore because believe me it's a big problem, it is a big problem. So you remember for about two weeks, I said, boy, this is tougher than I thought running for president. And then you found out this tremendous crime, there's tremendous drugs pouring across the border, tremendous beyond going to Chicago, going to

New York, going to LA going all over our country, so the drugs pour in and the money pours out, not a good deal. We get the drugs, they get the money, the drug cartels are going wild. They cannot believe how stupid our government is. They are making a fortune. The drugs come in, the money goes out daily and I saw it because I was on the border, I was there and we saw it and everybody sees it every day and we have the kind of people that can do something about it, but we have no leadership. None, none whatsoever. So we're, gonna build a wall and Mexico's gonna pay for the wall, believe me, you know, a lot of politicians that said, "oh, they're, not gonna pay", don't know anything about. They never read The Art of the Deal.

Speech in Los Angeles, California, September 15, 2015

ON THE IRAN NUCLEAR DEAL

We just don't see it, you know, you take a look at a thing like the Iran deal. We took freedom of religion, look at the Iran deal. How long is this whole thing gonna last when we have incompetent people. Grossly incompetent people, negotiating these vital deals like that deal we're 24 days and all you, I don't have to go over all of the many problems with the deal, even Israel, Israel is in such trouble with this deal, and you know, in that deal probably, it says and nobody even understands what it says, which is a problem. But probably if Israel ever attacked Iran we're supposed to come to their defense. Do we know that? Nobody's able to tell us what is going on with respect to that. If Israel has to, because, at some point, something might happen, the deal is horrible, the deal is horrible from any standpoint and we have to do something. And I can say it's got to have to be renegotiated. You know, I've made a living off buying bad -- I love bad deals because you buy them cheap. Do you understand that? you buy 'em cheap? I love horrible contracts. I love buying. I bought them from friends of mine. I buy a horrible, horrible contract, the poor guys dying with it, he's getting killed, I buy it cheap, I then go and fight like hell and make it a great contract. Sometimes you chapter it's something, you do lots of different things, whatever you have to do, and you make it a great contract. That contract, that agreement has to be changed. We have no choice because if it is it you're, gonna have nuclear proliferation, it's already happening, you're gonna have potentially the destruction of Israel. It has to be changed. One of the things in that contract, that I cannot believe, we're giving them $150 billion, billion. Right. Now we're giving them $150 billion, of which they're going to use, and already using, they've already -- they're ordering missiles from Russia. They're doing things that probably and definitely we can't allow them to do, but they're doing it. We cannot allow the incompetence that we've have going on in this country, we just can't. We have to use our greatest negotiators, we have to use our smartest people. We use political hacks, they're all political hacks, they're negotiating deals that they should have no right doing it.

Speech in Washington, D.C., September 25, 2015

ON HOUSEHOLD APPLIANCES

Every major Democrat running for president has pledged to eliminate gas-powered automobiles and destroy the U.S. auto industry forever, think of it. And you know why? Because they have these maniacs that say you got to go all-electric. I want to have an alternative, a big alternative, and you don't always have the alternative. And a lot of people don't know all of the electric can never catch the gas, you know. And by the way, there'll be different forms of energy coming along, but they want to close them up. And we're not closing them up. We're going to have lots of alternatives so that you can have it from a pricing, you can have it from a lot of different reasons. We're even bringing back the old light bulb. You heard about that, right? The old light bulb which is better. I say why do I always look so orange? You know why, because of the new light, they're terrible. You look terrible. They cost you many, many times more, like four or five times more. And you know, they're considered hazardous waste. When a light bulb is out, you've got to bring it to a dump. So let's say over here at Battle Creek, where's your nearest dump? OK, that's what, a couple of hundred miles away. So every time you lose, drive a couple of hundred miles. I said how many people do that? Nobody. What are they doing? They throw it in the garbage. But you know what it is because it's all gas. It's much more expensive, four or five times. When I came into office I did a lot of this. Sinks, showers, all of this stuff. I did a lot of it. The water comes out. You have areas where there's so much water you don't know what to do with it. You turn on the shower, you're not allowed to have any water anymore. I mean we do a lot of it. Dishwashers, we did the dishwasher, right? You press it -- remember the dishwasher, you press it, boom, they'd be like an explosion. Five minutes later, you open it up, the steam pours out the dishes. Now, you press it 12 times. Women tell me again, you know, they give you four drops of water. And they're in places where there's so much water they don't know what to do with it. So we just came out with a rag on dishwashers, we're going back to you. By the way, by the time they press it 10 times, you spend more on water and electric. Don't forget. The whole thing is worse because you're spending all that money on electric. So we're bringing back standards that are great and better machinery, but you can have the water again. But with the light bulb, I said what's going on with the light bulbs? So a lot of people are complaining about the cost, so I had a couple of experts come in. I said, tell me what gives a better light? Well, we like the old light bulb better. I said I like it better. And so what I did is, you could have either one. If you want to buy the newer kind, you can. And if you want to look very handsome or beautiful by buying the older kind like I do. So we're bringing back the old light bulb. So it's a much less expensive. It probably gives a better light, but whatever it is -- and you'll be able to spend a lot less money for a light bulb. I mean it sounds like little but it's big stuff. OK, it's big stuff. And we're doing it with a lot of other things, our dishwashers and, you know, I won't tell you one of the things because every time I tell you, they do a big number on it. You know, with the one I'm talking about, right? Sinks, right? Showers, and what goes with a sink and a shower? 10 times, right, 10 times. Bam, bam, not me, of course not me, but you -- him, but I never mentioned that because one time I mentioned all three, I said sinks, showers, and toilets. The headline was Trump with the toilets, toilets. That's all they were. They don't even mention that. So I didn't mention that. OK, I go off the record. But you know what, it's terrible. You want to wash your hands, you turn on the sink, no water comes out. So you leave the water, go 10 times as long, it's the same thing. You have a shower, it's no good for me.

Speech at political rally in Battle Creek, Michigan,
December 18, 2019

BIBLIOGRAPHY

Trump, Donald. "Speech: Donald Trump Holds a Campaign Rally in Hilton Head, SC - December 30, 2015". Factba.se, FactSquared, Inc., https://factba.se/transcript/donald-trump-speech-campaign-rally-hilton-head-sc-december-30-2015.

Trump, Donald. "Speech: Donald Trump Addresses the Turning Point USA Student Action Summit - December 21, 2019". Factba.se, FactSquared, Inc., https://factba.se/transcript/donald-trump-speech-turning-point-usa-student-summit-december-21-2019.

Trump, Donald. "Speech: Donald Trump Holds a Political Rally in Tulsa, Oklahoma - June 20, 2020". Factba.se, FactSquared, Inc., https://factba.se/transcript/donald-trump-speech-kag-rally-tulsa-oklahoma-june-20-2020.

Trump, Donald. "Speech: Donald Trump Delivers Address at the Kennedy Space Center After SpaceX Launch - May 30, 2020". Factba.se, FactSquared, Inc., https://factba.se/transcript/donald-trump-speech-nasa-spacex-launch-kennedy-space-center-may-30-2020.

Trump, Donald. "Remarks: Donald Trump Tours the Ford Rawsonville Plant in Ypsilanti, Michigan - May 21, 2020". Factba.se, FactSquared, Inc., https://factba.se/transcript/donald-trump-remarks-ford-plant-tour-ypsilanti-may-21-2020.

Trump, Donald. "Speech: Donald Trump Addresses the the World Economic Forum in Davos - January 21, 2020". Factba.se, FactSquared, Inc., https://factba.se/transcript/donald-trump-speech-world-economic-forum-davos-january-21-2020.

Trump, Donald. "Speech: Donald Trump Addresses the Evangelicals for Trump in Miami - January 3, 2020". Factba.se, FactSquared, Inc., https://factba.se/transcript/donald-trump-speech-evangelicals-for-trump-miami-january-3-2020.

Trump, Donald. "Speech: Donald Trump Addresses the International Association of Chiefs of Police -

October 28, 2019". Factba.se, FactSquared, Inc., https://factba.se/transcript/donald-trump-speech-international-police-chiefs-chicago-october-28-2019.

Trump, Donald. "Interview: Sean Hannity Hosts a Town Hall With Donald Trump in Green Bay, Wisconsin - June 25, 2020". Factba.se, FactSquared, Inc., https://factba.se/transcript/donald-trump-interview-town-hall-hannity-fox-news-marinette-wisconsin-june-25-2020.

Trump, Donald. "Speech: Donald Trump Delivers a Campaign Speech in Ames, IA - August 10, 2013". Factba.se, FactSquared, Inc., https://factba.se/transcript/donald-trump-speech-ames-ia-august-10-2013.

Trump, Donald. "Speech: Donald Trump Attends a Fourth of July Fireworks Show at Mount Rushmore - July 3, 2020". Factba.se, FactSquared, Inc., https://factba.se/transcript/donald-trump-speech-mount-rushmore-independence-day-july-3-2020.

Trump, Donald. "Speech: Donald Trump in Los

Angeles, CA - September 15, 2015". Factba.se, FactSquared, Inc., https://factba.se/transcript/donald-trump-speech-los-angeles-ca-september-15-2015.

Trump, Donald. "Speech: Donald Trump in Washington, DC - September 25, 2015". Factba.se, FactSquared, Inc., https://factba.se/transcript/donald-trump-speech-washington-dc-september-25-2015.

Trump, Donald. "Speech: Donald Trump Holds a Political Rally in Battle Creek, Michigan - December 18, 2019". Factba.se, FactSquared, Inc., https://factba.se/transcript/donald-trump-speech-kag-rally-battle-creek-mi-december-18-2019.

Printed in Great Britain
by Amazon

50450908R00035